# Pathways Through the Land of the Hart

Miriam Feinberg Vamosh

D1568628

gefen גפן
publishing house בית הוצאה לאור

*Photo Typeset by Gefen Ltd.*

*Cover Design by Helen Twena*

ISBN 965-229-089-0

Edition   9  8  7  6  5  4  3  2  1


Gefen Publishing House Ltd.          Gefen Books
POB 6056, Jerusalem                  12 New Street
91060 Israel                         Hewlett, N.Y., U.S.A. 11557

*Cover photo: Doron Horowitz*

Printed in Israel

*This volume is dedicated to the memory of
Nathan Amorai (1949-1990) — respected guide,
excellent matchmaker, beloved friend.*

# *Acknowledgments*

Many thanks to Mike and Jill Rogoff for their gracious help and encouragement, and to text editor Elizabeth Harris. My deepest appreciation and love go to my parents, Milton and Danessa Feinberg, for their unswerving support in the realization of this work, and for setting me on the path, and to my husband Aharon who walks it with me.

# Table Of Contents

# Introduction

A thousand sacred stories from the ancient and tumultuous Book of Books speak to us of a Land we have never seen, yet one we know as well as we know the soil of our own birthplace. It is an undeniable fact that in the spiritual lives of people everywhere who love the Bible, some part of the Land, its marshes or its mountains, its deserts or its tropics, its snowy heights, rocky crags or rushing rivers, will always seem like home to someone, somewhere in the world.

Historians, botanists and geographers have written volumes to explain this fact. They expound upon the unique location of the Holy Land. They speak of a bridge between continents bringing emissaries from far-flung lands and cultures together to change the history of the world. They catalog plants, both African and Alpine, that flourish together in this one tiny corner of the globe. For the pilgrim, however, these facts have significance beyond the scholarly: This Land was intended to be a reflection of the whole world.

Come now to the Land. In the marvelous diversity of its physical features, find that link to your own homeland, and forge a new one — accept it as your spiritual birthplace, for in this soil the ageless wisdom of the Bible first found expression. Sing here with the psalmist of the richness of the Land. Rejoice with the prophets in the fulfilment of their visions of redemption of the Land and of its exiled people.

But when time and distance take their toll, what will tie you to the sights and sounds you have vowed never to forget? In the whirlwind of your journey, in the crush and flurry of new experience, you sensed so many thoughts that were diffused before you could speak them, found images that tugged at your sleeve, then rushed away before you could turn. The landscape that inspired psalmist and prophet can be so humble, all too often pushed aside by the crowd of glittering monuments and ruined avenues vying for your attention.

The memories are there. They will await your solitude and your dreaming hours, to be summoned and contemplated without distraction. Perhaps the thoughts and images within these pages will reflect some of your own special moments, moments of oneness with the eternal inspiration of this Land. And when you open this book, they will step out and embrace you like an old friend from whom you have been sadly, reluctantly, parted.

# Oasis

The oasis and the desert are locked in eternal struggle. The oasis is the antithesis of the desert, and the desert takes its revenge with incessant encroachment. Here the essential is revealed, here lies the boundary between life and death.

And in this place human beings may have first discovered their Creator. On the glaring slopes above the Ein Gedi spring lie the ruins of a 6,000 year old temple. Was it dedicated in some distant yesteryear to the very God who produced this haven of greenery in the barrenness? At Jericho, where water and climate combine to produce some of the richest land of the ancient world, traces of early human burials have been unearthed. In the carefully prepared skulls laid reverently beneath the house floors is evidence of belief in the afterlife, prolog to an understanding of the Eternal Spirit.

At the oasis human beings must have deduced what to them was surely the earth's most carefully guarded secret: scattered seed will produce food year after year in the place where it is sown and tended. From the moment of that discovery, they devised elaborate rituals through which they beseeched some deity to increase the yield of their land and protect them from the ravages of nature. They found that the blessing of the freely, sometimes fiercely flowing waters, cascading upon them from the mountain ridge above, could be channeled, and cause the rich, alluvial earth to produce even more abundantly.

When the greenly clad earth at Jericho or Ein Gedi smiles and gives endlessly of her bounty, it is almost possible to forget what lies further to the south. Beyond the Dead Sea is a valley where nothing seems to take root — in that place, the Bible says, fire and brimstone rained down death and destruction on a paradise. The land indeed looks to have been cloaked with a suffocating mantle of white, sterile ash. The turquoise sea slashes Judah from Moab, his long-lost ancestor. Invitingly, its surface reflects the ocher mountains, but its depths, infused with burning salts and minerals, silently suffer

Sodom's curse. Under an unrelenting sun, the salty pillars and islands, congealed from the waters, look uncannily, mockingly, like ice-floes.

Humanity has made the difference here, changing the face of the sea, its very name discouraging. From the Dead Sea waters comes life: potash which fertilizes and regenerates the soil of far and hungry corners of the globe, and minerals which are a balm for various human ailments.

The story of this Land, the strength of its fecundity set against the howling of its wastelands, its natural oases and oases born of human toil, is one with the story of the never-ending struggle for life.

## Land of the Hart

Of all the names bestowed upon the Land of Israel, none is more lovely, yet less familiar, than "Land of the Hart". In vain do we search for it in translations of the Bible. Look to Jeremiah 3:19,

> *How gladly would I treat you like sons and give you a desirable land, the most beautiful inheritence of the nations.*

Or Daniel 11:41,

> *At the time of the end (the king of the north) will invade many countries. He will also invade the beautiful land. He will pitch his tent between the seas and the beautiful holy mountain.*

Or II Samuel 1:19,

> *Your beauty O Israel, lies slain on your heights. How the mighty have fallen!*

The image is there, though disguised beyond recognition by the translator. Were we able to immerse ourselves in the Hebrew original, thus would Jeremiah speak for God:

> *How gladly would I treat you like sons and give you a desirable land, the inheritance of the hart.*

Daniel would prophesy:

> *... He will also invade the land of the hart. He will pitch his tent between the sea and the holy mountain of the hart.*

And David would lament the death of Saul and Jonathan with these words:
*The hart, Israel, lies slain on your heights. How the mighty have fallen!*

Adorned with their original significance, these verses now convey new depth and meaning, and we wonder at the translators of the Bible, who have deprived us of so striking an image. Perhaps, laboring in distant lands, they were unable to conceive of the Holy Land in this guise. Likening a corner of the earth to a small relative of the deer is indeed a strange simile, yet a potent one. We are touched by its singularity and we are moved to ask, with the ancient rabbis, "Why is the Land of Israel like a hart"?

The highlands of Canaan belonged to the hart. In large numbers it roamed free in the mountains where human presence was almost unknown. As it watched silently from the midst of the tangled oaks, the hart bequeathed its inheritance to another: the Israelites came upon the land, cleared it for cultivation, and transformed its image, and the face of history, forever. But the hart is only one of the many creatures at home in the landscape of ancient and present-day Israel. Its significance as a symbol does not stem from its mere presence; so much about this graceful animal truly embodies the essence of the Land.

The Land of Israel is subtle. It does not march noisily from season to season riotously changing its raiment as summer turns to fall, or winter to spring. The changing of seasons here is delicate, deliberate. The earth senses every nuance. Even the barest scent of moisture brings forth the crocus and the seasquill, harbingers of autumn. Long before our human senses are aware, the Land has changed its hue and winter is upon us.

The hart, too, is finely tuned in harmony with its surroundings. A barely perceptible movement on the outer reaches of its field of vision, a minute difference in the air's scent, and the hart's trembling response is quickened. We, who rely so ponderously upon our five senses, cannot begin to comprehend the warnings that animate the hart.

The fragile fertility of the Land husbanding its resources, the enhanced sensitivity of the animal endangered: thus those who exist on the edge of existence endure.

The hart lays no claim to glorious colors, imposing size, or trumpeting call. The hart's beauty is in its subtlety, its substance recognized in afterthought: only when it has sped away do we realize that we have witnessed a creature as ephemeral as the air it has leapt through to escape us.

And so the Land. Where is its magnificence? Not in broad rushing rivers or in mighty mountain ranges, but in the shadows lengthening across a russet slope where it meets the improbable salt sea, or in the radiance of a sunrise across the dun vastness of the wilderness. One who can find grace in these will find satisfaction of the soul in the elusive beauty of the hart.

Though it has a tremendous will to survive, the hart is often the victim of some hungry predator. Its only recourse is to escape and seek refuge, to wait for the time of strength and the season of rebirth that will replenish its depleted numbers. The Land too has few defenses. Its soil has churned under the heavy tread of countless enemies, like the flesh of the hart, torn from its bones by unrelenting fangs. The Land too waits, fallen and deserted, for the day of rebirth, of redemption.

Daniel reminds us that in the midst of the Land of the Hart there is holiness. What is this holiness? The more we desire to know it, the more it seems to recede from our grasp, like the hart on the hoof, disappearing over the horizon. The Land is the beloved of God, and so it is called holy. It is in our search for insight, in our desire to discern yet another facet of its mysterious attraction, that we approach the essence of its sanctity, and manifest our love for the Eternal.

# Masada

The great stronghold towers overhead. Conceived as a last royal refuge, no resource was spared in constructing its ingenious water system, or in stocking its immense storehouses and armories.

The builder of Jerusalem's dazzling Temple and the opulent show-case city of Caesarea did not envision Masada, despite its desolate location, as a spartan encampment. The great Herod ordered it to be graced with every amenity. An impossible three-tiered palace was suspended from its northern face. Luscious gardens and luxuriously appointed baths became a legend in their time. Untold cost and effort changed the face of the mountain: man's ingenuity strained to the breaking point in this improbable abode.

Herod's engineering feats have endured two millennia and still astound all who behold them. And so the first view of Masada, sharply outlined in the distance against the desert sky, makes us eager to hear more of the incomparable builder-King of Judea, of his unbridled pride, his glorious achievements, and the horrific consequences of his reign.

As we draw closer, we watch Masada cast its imperious shadow over a neighborhood of odd formations nearly extending to the sea. Considering what we already know of the creation overhead we are quick to draw conclusions about their nature. They stand, row upon row, undoubtedly the product of expert planning by an accomplished engineer. Their polychrome layered surfaces could only have been the work of an experienced architect, anxious to please a demanding royal patron. It is easy to picture a grand retinue of lords and ladies, leaving these palaces to be borne up the mountain for an elegant soirée.

Palaces, indeed?

Something is not quite right about our imaginary neighborhood of noblemen. A second glance leaves us with the feeling that our first impression is about to be dispelled. And, in fact, when we have reached the height of the fortress and are looking out over the plain, our perspective is entirely different, and the riddle is solved.

From above, there can be no mistake. These are no builder's fantasies. They are the very desert itself, created and recreated out of the floodwaters that burst each winter from the canyons of the Judean wilderness.

The ageless symmetry of these formations makes a mockery out of all the efforts on the rocky fortress above them. These plateaus are still alive, still changing. Water, their chief architect, is still hard at work evolving extraordinary patterns, which we in our folly believe impossible of nature. So enticed are we by tales of greatness a mere two thousand years old that we believe those ancients capable of anything. We even mistake for human effort the unbounded energy of nature's forces.

We build and create, but we would need thousands of hands to merely approximate the perfection of the natural world. Momentarily we may even confuse the grandest of human achievement with that perfection. Yet we must realize in the end that nature is a quantum leap beyond anything the human mind can envision. Masada and its "palaces" help teach us that lesson: they are the meeting place of the everlasting and the temporal.

*The oasis of Jericho*

## Harts: Israel's gazelles
Doron Horowitz (Nature Reserves Authority)

*Masada, with marl formations in the foreground*                    Roy Brody

*Negev landscape*   JNF Archives

*Sea of Galilee at dusk*   Government Press Office

# Light

The first force of Creation — stimulating the most powerful of our senses. It identifies, defines and colors. Light grants us access to the world. It is essential to our very being. Yet light is such a prosaic part of our everyday lives that we are certain it cannot surprize us. Neither glowing shades of evening, nor pastel dawn, nor the sparkle of sun-diamonds on water moves us any longer. So we assume. Until we meet the light anew, in the Land. It is then that we discover another dimension to this most familiar of all experiences.

Standing before the Western Wall in the brief moment of dusk, we are witness to a strange phenomenon. The stones are suffused with a glow which seems to emanate from within. We are no longer merely observing the last rays of another sunlit Jerusalem day reflected upon the stone. For as the sun's rays lengthen, from gold to rose, deeper and deeper, we too have become suffused with that glow of other-worldly incandescence. Sounds which distracted us but a moment before fall silent, and a soft breeze stirs. At this enchanted hour we are suspended between heaven and earth, and touched with the mystery that is Jerusalem. Thus Jerusalem's luster must have touched our ancestors through the generations, moving them to poetry and song, and sometimes to weeping. We are one with them at this hour, and we are filled with awe.

The changing light at the Sea of Galilee seems neither dependent on time of day, nor season of the year. At times an azure sky is reflected in an unimaginable blue below. The shadows over Galilee's eastern shore outline the mountains at the water's edge, turning them into gnarled, loving fingers, gripping the water's edge. This is the lake of forgiveness, of renewal, of inner peace.

Then, in a moment, the mood of the lake will change. It turns into an angry, impenetrable sheet, eerily silent under a white sky. There is tension in the air, and the region's graceful beauty retreats into oblivion. In the briefest of moments the lake has trapped absolution, as well as light, beneath its now-grim waters. We can sense the sadness of the unhealed and the unforgiven.

In days gone by, thousands flocked to these sacred shores to beg respite from their misery. To one who approaches the lake now with a seeking heart, the changing of the light is a reminder of the joy and sorrow of those long-ago supplicants. It is a mirror of response — a reflection of the emotion that wells up when we know that our prayers have been answered, or with equal certainty that our petition has been denied.

Safed: Perched in the hills high above the Sea of Galilee, this town has been recognized since Medieval times as the home of Jewish mysticism. Here scholars plumbed the hidden wisdom of the Bible to know the will of God, and sought the path to perfect harmony with the universe. Safed's narrow lanes and tiny houses are a wash of blue and white, gleaming like pearls in the Galilee sun. Light cascades through arching windows and doors, collecting in the alleyways in bright pools or in tranquilly shifting patterns of shade. Wherever we turn, the light works its magic, now revealing, now concealing, all-pervasive yet selective. Wandering its streets, we begin to understand how the sages of Safed were drawn to create a parallel between light and its source, between the Creator and His handiwork: that which changes all it touches, yet remains unchanged, radiates endless energy yet remains undiminished, the unfathomable source of all existence. By these characteristics of light, which a moment's pause in a mystic's hideaway has allowed us to perceive, we become closer to these same attributes as they exist in the Creator. Sparks of glory have been revealed to us.

In the desert, light rules unflinchingly over the Land and its inhabitants. The light here is direct, brilliant, even painful. Unfiltered by the great swaths of green covering the nakedness of the earth in more gentle climates, every feature of the landscape is transfigured at their command. The Land casts off one form and wears another, in obedience to the cadence of the sun's march across the sky.

Only dawn in the desert shows tenderness, with the compassion of the first light. It sends the predators of the night into their lairs, and their prey ventures forth without fear, to feast upon the still dewy plants or to quench their thirst at the spring. By midday the desert is the harshest of masters, shimmering in a white-hot, merciless glare, granting no reprieves. When darkness finally descends, it is almost without warning. No lingering dusk here, the light is torn away in an instant.

Here there can be no compromise, no indecision. And so it was that the prophets sought out the rigors of the desert, as severe and exacting as the Source of their visions, to inspire and fortify them in bearing the burden of their message.

The light here has become entwined with every fiber of our consciousness. Light has been our teacher and constant companion, allowing us to enjoy the beauty of varied landscapes. But the light has granted us much more than a simple awareness of our physical surroundings. Light has enhanced our perception of sanctity in the places of our pilgrimage. Its power has illuminated our spirit. In its ebb and flow, its giving and taking, light has opened our eyes to the acknowledgement of the omnipotent Prime Mover of the Universe.

## The Donkey

You know me well, although we have not, as yet, met face to face. And what bizarre circumstances for a first meeting with the one you thought to encounter with distinction, as I appear in the pages of your Bible. Yet here I stand, amidst the fumes and the slippery wetness of the petrol station, taking on kerosene from the pump. The shock of seeing me thus for the first time will make you laugh, I know. You joke about my "filling up my tanks" as you would speak of your more dignified forms of transportation. Well, I find nothing amusing about it, I must tell you. I am, as always, the bearer of the burden, this time the agent of warmth to winter homes. The donkey at the petrol station...what a long way I have come!

No plodder I, and he who calls me slow maligns me. The heels of my rider, nearly hidden by clouds of dust, drag low on the ground as together we race, hoof upon heel, hoof upon heel. I am known by my bray, that sharp, screeching, impossible intake of air which echoes fiercely between high stone walls. It is then that I mournfully recall other times and places, and a grandeur shared with no other denizen of the animal kingdom.

Balaam rode forward on a donkey's back, blind to the glory that shone in his path. It was one of my kind who perceived the angel that day and signaled its presence with a human voice. Zachariah envisioned the heights attained by the King Messiah entering Jerusalem, not astride my proud and prancing cousin the horse, but on the swaying back of the smallest beast of burden.

Jesus of Nazareth had a wealthy man's tomb and counted the affluent among His disciples. A litter, a dashing steed, even the shoulders of the devoted could have carried Him into Jerusalem. Yet, remembering Zachariah, He chose one of my ancestors to bear Him down the Mount of Olives to His fate. And when I am at rest, my dusty back unbound, I still bear one burden: legend has marked the memory of that day in the dark and furry cross draped upon my shoulders.

I trudge disparaged from task to task these days, and only those to whom I am a novelty even notice my existence or recall those better times. Regard me with mirth, or pity me if you must. But you who come from afar, remember: I am one who could see and speak of visions, who bore the burden of prophets and kings. And cherish me a little, too.

# The Greatest of Blessings

*How good and how pleasant it is when*
*brothers dwell together in unity!*
*...It is as if the dew of Hermon*
*were falling on Mt. Zion.*
*For there the Lord bestows his blessing,*
*even life forever more.*

Psalm 133

These words of the psalmist, recited and sung in numerous languages, attest to our unrequited yearning for peace and love in a world torn with strife. But it is when we look beyond the exuberant first verse to the simile, steeped in the natural beauty of the Land so familiar to the psalmist, that we truly grasp the significance of these well-loved phrases.

In lands where water is plentiful, where streams, rivers, pools and ponds compete on nature's stage, it is difficult to imagine the importance of "dew" to the dry land of the Bible. In the southland of Israel, the Negev, land of rocky sun-scorched mountains and parched riverbeds, the ancient desert dwellers treated the dew as nature's greatest gift. In areas where no spring waters could ever reach, they would form piles of rocks and train grapevines to trail over them. The precious dawn mist would pool in the shade created by the rocks before the broiling sun rose high enough to burn it away. The grapes drank and flourished, bursting with their juice.

The careful conservation of meager water resources in the Negev produced dramatic results for the inhabitants of that parched region. But in the north, the picture is far different, for here the Land is blessed with a perennial water source, the "dew of Hermon". Mt. Hermon majestically reigns above the Huleh valley, at that meeting place of mountains, Galilee to the west and Golan to the east. Old King Hermon turns the freezing snows that are his mantle into rivers which cascade down the slopes. Three raging sons, vying for this inheritance, the Banias, the Dan, and the Hatzbani, finally unite to form the Jordan. Before rushing headlong to its rendezvous with the Dead Sea, to disappear in salty disappointment, the Jordan fills the basin of the Sea of Galilee, providing the Land and its thirsty inhabitants with the gift of life: sweet waters. No wonder that even in modern times Hermon was deemed "father of all waters". Through the "dew of Hermon", the Land revelled in fulfilment of promise and prophecy.

Our psalmist of old brought to his immortal poetry a deep understanding of the contrasts in the Land, its capriciousness of some water resources and the abundant flow of others. Yet his knowledge embraced much more than just the topography and climate of his homeland; he had a deep insight into human nature. He understood that though our thirst may be quenched and our pastures green, we may never be truly content unless our spiritual needs also find their fulfilment.

And so he invoked Jerusalem's most ancient name, Zion: site of the Temple, metaphor of the spiritual. He revealed his vision of hope in our frail human existence, dependent as it is on nature's vagaries and the yearnings of our soul. That vision sees the meeting of our physical and spiritual needs in one and the same place, "the dew of Hermon falling on Mt. Zion". Peaceful coexistence, the psalmist teaches, as if neither our bodies nor our souls need ever thirst again, is the apex of all we could ever desire.

# To Love a City

How do Jerusalem's chiseled stones come to evoke the love we feel for this city?

The spirited streets push against me on all sides, slowing my gait and drawing me into their life-beat. My pilgrim's climb up endless steps quickens my heart and awakens my soul. Removing my shoes as custom demands in a high and ancient place, I feel the flagstones beneath my feet, warm in the midday sun. Yet their same touch can chill me to the bone in the grey days of winter. The stones, in their fusion of frost and fire, command, and I am rooted to them.

I can close my eyes in this city and know that I can be nowhere else. The clink of the stonemason's chisel is constant, I hear its echoes resounding down through time. The handiwork of thousands of years still stands, and the work continues, the endless building. My fingertips trace the chipped stone faces and my mind's eye surveys the glories of ages past. I understand at once the need for the builders to share in this city.

Eyes shut, I can recognize Jerusalem by other sounds. Where else but here would the dusk of Sabbath-eve bring a wailing siren announcing the day of rest, the yearning call of the muezzin from a dozen minarets, and church bells tolling vespers, in simultaneous, cacophonous competition?

Yes, I feel love for this city, a strong and binding love, because it captures, awakens, embraces the senses. Each step I take, each time I lift my eyes, it draws me inward and reflects my desires, my warmth, my cold places. The past and future generations I carry within me, seek it, speak to its eternal soul, and I am the medium.

## The Gate Of Mercy

Gate of Mercy, we called your name, as we implored you to open before us, to grant our eyes a glimpse of Jerusalem, no longer our own. But mercy was not yours to bestow. Only on that one day each year, the anniversary of the destruction, were we permitted to stand within your elegant halls. We could not drink in your beauty, for our eyes were veiled with sadness. Our wailing rose to your vaulted roof and the echoes of our lamentations swirled around us. When dusk fell, you cruelly shut us out. Our backs turned to the warmth of redemption, we again thrust our faces against the cold wind of exile.

Wherever we wandered, we wove the memories of our keening beneath your domes, into the walls and archways of our houses of prayer. Thus we carried you within, and when we raised our eyes to pray for Jerusalem rebuilt, there above us appeared the arches of the sealed and sorrowful gate. There were times when as pilgrims, nearly broken, our flagging spirits were revived with the first sight of your double threshold to our heart's desire. We approached, and were turned away. We sank to the ground before you, and our prayers were as the mewling of lion cubs before the fallen body of their mother. And we called your name, Gate of No Mercy.

Anguish was our portion there, but there also we garnered our strength. When we sang with the psalmist, "our feet are standing within thy gates", we sang not of our physical presence in the city, for others granted or denied us access according to their whim. Rather, we sang of Jerusalem, the healer: When we were within your gates, even if only in a vision, we stood, we stood strong and fast. That strength was our succor when Jerusalem was but a memory and an unattainable dream.

Despair is not the end of this tale. Your other names ring out for those who listen, and charge the air with expectation. For the Muslims, you are the Gate of Eternal Life. Generations of their dead are gathered around you on the hillside in anticipation of the day they call The Awakening. To the Christians, you are the Golden, the royal gate, built to welcome the Messiah. Jews saw in your double arches the ancient Gate of Bridegrooms and Mourners. Passing through one meant good wishes for the future, through the other, comfort in the hour of loss.

In this at least, in the naming of the gate for the dearest aspirations of humankind, the warring traditions of Moses and Mohammed find themselves united. It is this harmony of hopes, this longing for concord, that will one day open the gate forever.

And so we call your name, Gate of Mercy of the Days to Come.

*18th Century engraving of the interior of the Gate of Mercy*
Jerusalem Municipal Archives

*The Gate of Mercy today, on the eastern side of Jerusalem's 16th Century Old City Wall*
Aharon Vamosh

*Beast of burden*

Courtesy Mike Rogoff

*Lake Hulah with snow-capped Mt. Hermon in the distance*
Miriam Feinberg Vamosh

*Water conservation techniques, like this dam, perfected by the Nabateans nearly 2,000 years ago, enabled them to cultivate the Negev*
JNF Archives

*The Mount of Olives by moonlight*

Ministry of Tourism Archives

## Monumental Faith

Conquered innumerable times, Jerusalem's valleys filled with the rubble of the ages, her hills with the echoes of ancient praise. Generations of neglect by her absentee landlords finally took their toll, ruin and privation reigning over the city. Here was a void, calling out to be filled. And when sailing ships turned to steam and thousands rode the rail, they answered the call. They pounded Jerusalem's shores like a high tide, changing her forever.

They came from afar, with dreams of ruling the world from her high places. The crowned heads of Europe turned as one eastward. They sought a new name for their tempting and compelling discovery: they called it the Middle East. They took their places at the edges of a great new gaming board at whose center was a gleaming goal: Jerusalem. Their pawns were the ancient stewards of the holy places, almost forgotten until this time of change. Thus, communities of dismally quartered monks became purveyors of temporal power for European patrons.

Jerusalem's native sons looked on in amazement as ornate French balustrades, rows of Russian windows, and high Bavarian turrets came to dominate the decay and desolation. Steeples pierced a skyline once ruled by the light and airy dome. From their homelands volumes of letters and armies of emissaries came to cheer on the Europeans of the new Jerusalem. Build on! Build higher, stronger than the rest! Choose your site prudently, sustain its gardians so they will bear your interests faithfully above all others and immortalize your name. They bid for the grandest view, and vied for the heights. "Out of the depths I call upon you, O Lord". The psalmist would not know these many-garrisoned peaks. He would not recognize Jerusalem's feuding potentates, striving one against the other to please a distant, earthly master.

Princes poured out their coffers to grace the hills. Yet if they journeyed to the scene of their grand designs, it was to laud the builders or to lay a cornerstone, only to retreat once again across the seas. They rarely stayed to witness the fulfilment of their dreams. Confident that their Jerusalem was secure, they left their properties to be tended by an odd assemblage of expatriates and their local retinue.

The time came when the world was engulfed by war. Power and fortunes shifted. There was no hand to reach out and claim these giant follies, crouching heavily on the hills. The windows of the fortresses darkened. Their grim, deserted shells mocked the aims of their designers — more absentee landlords for Jerusalem. Some were rendered useful in ways never envisioned by their architects, and new tenants walked their cavernous halls. The buildings became sad sentinels in an encampment of ruin, as a dozen battles raged around them, wounding and battering their facades.

Generations have passed. The princes are no more; their power has passed on, into other hands. The children's children of their subjects are now pilgrims, unencumbered by delusion, with humbler goals. When they gaze at Jerusalem's monumental foreign landmarks, so similar to the grand architecture of their homelands, they sense a familiarity of line and style that can only say, you are at home here. They feel the welcome of a long-lost relative with a family resemblance so strong that none can deny the bond. Once outlandish expressions of arrogance, then the saddest of ruins, today restored, these structures are now intrinsically Jerusalem. They take their place in the eternal drama that is this city, of which stones and mortar are the metaphor. Through these sites wayfarers from every corner of the earth become part of the Holy City.

This was the vision of the prophet Isaiah: "It will be raised above the hills, and all nations shall flow unto it..."

## The Dome of the Rock

Islam embraced faith in a God who created human beings in His image, but denied them the right to depict that image in human form. Submission to this discipline freed Islamic artists to explore new realms of expression of spirituality. I am not a Muslim, and upon entering the Dome of the Rock, I come face to face with a world of symbols — unfamiliar, yet to which I feel an immediate kinship. The search for the perfect way to acknowledge the Divine beckons to me.

I lift my eyes to the Dome and surrender myself to the illusion of being lifted upwards — upwards to Paradise. An abundance of green fills my vision, so unlike the barren earth of Islam's Arabian birthplace. Here and there, the blue of the sky, daylight ever-present, keep the evils and uncertainty of the night at bay. Fruits hang heavy on every vine. Their names are unknown to me, for they are the fruits of Paradise, known only to the just, who have been relieved of their earthly burdens.

The soft curves of the intertwining vines give way to angles, geometric riddles which challenge my concentration. I follow them this way and that, finally discerning a pattern of expansion, bound only by the edges of the structure it decorates. I am grateful to this people, ancient masters of mathematics and astronomy, who found in the exactness of science a unique expression of the infinity of God.

Islam excelled not only in science, but also gave the world an art form: the Arabesque. The letters of the Arabic alphabet, in the service of the Divine, are transformed into a flowing river whose eddies are words of wisdom and whose currents, attributes of God. Though I do not understand the meaning of the lines and strokes, I too immerse myself in this river merely by crossing the threshold. What a joy, to enter the place of worship and be immediately surrounded by this lexicon of praise!

One note, just one, tempers my exuberance over the unparalleled beauty and grace of this home of the spirit. It is the glint which catches my eye in this garden of mosaic flora. I learn that this is the glitter of decorative trophies, jewels pried from the crowns of dethroned monarchs who bent their knee to the conquerer. There is shock in the realization that this magnificent dome, pinnacle of aesthetic achievement, enshrines not only the triumph of the spirit, but also our instincts for warfare and conquest.

And there is sadness in being so close to the word of God, and so far from His design for Creation.

# Out of the North

*Out of the north, evil shall break forth.*

Jeremiah 1:14

These are the words of the fiery prophet who bore witness to the downfall of Jerusalem 2,500 years ago. They ring true not only for Jeremiah, but also for a world rent asunder by the conflicts of our own era.

Though these words were first spoken far from our homelands, they seem to have traversed history, crossing the world to reach out to us. They still hold meaning for us, for our European ancestors looked north with a fear of their own. It could have been Alfred the Great, long-ago king of the Anglo-Saxons, who uttered this prophecy. Vigilant on some rocky promontory of England's northern shore, eyes narrowed against the biting wind, he probed the mist for the silently gliding prow of a Viking craft that would signal yet another raid on the exhausted flock over which he ruled. Or consider the Gauls, ancestral inhabitants of France. When their chieftains met in council they were united in one chilling premonition: "Out of the north, evil shall break forth". Here was a Gallic nobleman speaking, warning of the dreaded Celtic invasion from across the water, of the destruction of crops his people had sown, but would never reap, of children stolen away to the northern wastelands of the invader. And who in those times doubted the power of the mighty Norse gods whose breath created the icy winds of winter, hardening the earth into frozen tundra never to be broken, even for burial of the dead?

Certainty of impending peril from the north has become a part of our European heritage. But the immortal expression of this certainty has been passed down to us neither from Norse mythology nor from the hoary history of England or France. It is

33

from the Bible. When Jeremiah spoke these words, his thoughts were of Jerusalem imperiled. It was a Jerusalem he knew well, for he came from a small village about a half-day's walk north of the city. He must have often entered the Holy City from this direction, and he knew too where invading armies thundering out of their northern lands would mount their attack: at the northern exposure, where Jerusalem's natural defenses are weakest.

Jerusalemites of old surely looked north with trepidation. For on all sides but this, deep valley-arms embraced their city, ensuring that no one could approach her ramparts undetected or scale them unscathed. And there, in the north, no valley at all, only the land sloping gently, ominously, towards the ramparts. If a determined attacker approached from the northern side, Jerusalem was doomed. So said the prophet, "I am bringing disaster from the north, even terrible destruction".

 Dramatic evidence of the fulfilment of Jeremiah's prophecy has been uncovered. The remains of great walls, and the weapons of both defenders and attackers, unearthed by archeologists, are testimony to the heroic but futile attempts to protect the vulnerable north. Assyrians, Babylonians, Greeks, Romans, Crusaders, all battered these magnificent defenses to ruin, and marched triumphant through Jerusalem's bleeding streets.

The north. In the end, merely a direction on the compass, a cold wind, or a quirk of topography. How strange that it should stir such similar emotions in peoples separated by half a world, and thousands of years. We are not the children of Jeremiah's Jerusalem, who suffered exile and defeat at the hands of northern enemies, but something deep within us communes with them. With mysterious accuracy, the Bible story is our story. We speak with one voice, hear the same cries, dread the same evils.

In this as in all ways, the Bible is a mirror for the universality of human experience.

## Thoughts on Mount Zion

Mt. Zion is among the most humble of hills, with almost indistinguishable characteristics. Yet pilgrims flow incessantly to its heights, for here is the tomb of one who is revered by three religions as prophet, king, and saint, and at the same time excoriated in Scripture as murderer, adulterer, and bandit. He is King David.

On the same hill there is a scarred patch of earth, an archeological excavation crowned by a church, known in Latin as "Peter in Gallicantu". Here, it is said, was the house of the High Priest, Caiaphas. To this spot, the New Testament relates, Jesus was brought for questioning. This may have been the scene of one of the most wrenching chapters of the Passion story, the denial of Jesus by his disciple Peter.

On Mt. Zion some of the most ignoble episodes of the Bible may be recalled, yet their protagonists — though prey to human error — were to be crowned in turn by both Judaism and Christianity. Mt. Zion links two men of antiquity to one of the most important ideas of our Judeo-Christian tradition: forgiveness.

David: a man of fiery emotions and impetuous desires. He could dance before the Ark of the Lord with joyous abandon and sing rapturous songs of praise to God, then descend into a bleak place of misery and despair at the recognition of his shortcomings and the devastation that was their fruit.

His actions caused the deaths of many, from his own flesh and blood — the infant child of Bathsheba, to thousands of innocents in the wake of his arrogant census of the fighting men. Yet Nathan the prophet assured him that God would spare his own life and make his house great. And it is to the tomb of this most human of humans, on the summit of Mt. Zion, that the faithful throughout the ages have come to invoke his name, asking him alone to bring their petitions before the Highest Throne.

A streak of instability cursed Peter, like David, and brought him to the brink of ruin more than once. Peter, at Jesus' side from the beginning, should have foreseen the inevitability of the end; at Caesarea Philippi, Peter was the first to testify to the messianic mission of Jesus. But Peter protested the cruel conclusion of that mission. And for this transgression, he who had been held in the highest regard, blessed and charged with leadership, is castigated in the very next breath. How Peter must have cringed to hear the stinging epithet Jesus flung his way, "Satan". At Gethsemane, this time by violent means, Peter tried to delay the fate of Jesus, earning himself a stern rebuke. Was Peter's impetuous and bloody act, cutting off the ear of the High Priest's guard, a belated attempt to defend the master whom he had abandoned for sleep on that night of all nights?

Peter's most damnable act could instead have been one of great bravery. The denial of his alliance with Jesus left his friend completely vulnerable at the hour when his unswerving support was most needed. Peter broke faith, and acted dishonorably. The church bearing his name which rises up from the slopes of Mt. Zion does not allow us to forget this, and is decorated with mosaic scenes recalling the violence, anger and betrayal that are the hallmark of that night.

But the other, contrasting images in that same church are the ones that remain with us: the tranquil shades of blue and green that depict moving scenes of sinners forgiven, and of Peter, enthroned, absolved of his disgrace.

David and Peter, each in his own way, return from the abyss. David mourns and cannot be comforted following the death of his son, Absalom. Wracked with despair, he is ready to rescind all that he has accomplished. But finally he is persuaded to assume the mantle of leadership once again, and takes his seat of authority in the gateway. When Jesus appeared to Peter on the shores of the Sea of Galilee, Peter's agony over his faithlessness was still a fresh wound. Yet Jesus reconsecrated him there. And so at

Pentecost on Mt. Zion, in the very shadow of David's tomb, Peter too resumes his task, addressing his listeners as the undisputed leader of the community.

There is a legend embroidered on the velvet cloth covering David's cenotaph: "David, King of Israel, lives on!" And as from Mt. Zion's peak we gaze out at the Jerusalem David founded, and the city where his descendent will someday reign, we realize his spirit is still with us, and his kingship was not annulled. At David's tomb, and in the church named after Peter, we are reminded that in the end these two great men overcame the dark places in their souls. They reached out in prayer and praise, and found forgiveness. Their stories go forth from Zion, and imbue us all with hope.

## The Spirit of Ruth

The silent tawny desert is endlessly reflected in her black eyes. Her mountain home is far behind her now, shimmering in the searing heat to which she has descended, as in a dream. Poised between two mountains, in the cleft between Moab and Judah, she resolutely turns her back upon the old and at that moment is born into the new. The descent is complete. Ruth ascends to her destiny.

The dust is thick upon her lashes and her mouth has dried with its taste upon her tongue. This is the last desert sunrise for Ruth. Its golden rays are cast upon the ridge of ripening barley fields above her, and her weary pace quickens at the first view of her journey's goal: harbinger of respite, cool stone dwellings, secure storehouses, wells of sweet water: fringed garment of the desert — Bethlehem, house of bread.

Here Ruth found a land of unparalleled tenacity. Its grain fields cling to the terraces reaching down to the very edge of the wilderness, denying the power of the barren expanses. So Ruth clung to Naomi, and with a great and ardent passion, to her adopted people. She challenged and redeemed the wasteland of her widowhood, ascending from the wilderness to the settled land.

Ruth lived out her life here, on the frontier of the infertile steppe, where existence depended on the tireless efforts of the villagers to wrest this fragile strip of cultivated land from a desert unwilling to concede the victory. Often she took her sons and her daughters, and then her grandchildren, out to the eastern brow of the hills, There amidst the green, yet perilously close to the arid habitation of the jackal and the scorpion, she taught them never to give in, either to the elements or to the raiding desert dwellers who would steal their hard-won harvest. She moved them to be like the land that embraced their village, determined and vital in the face of extinction.

Tales such as these are not soon forgotten, and from strength such as Ruth's, nations are forged. The spirit of Ruth lived on, invigorating the generations that followed her.

The son of her grandson, son of Bethlehem, the shepherd David, would take up her challenge. The enormous task of molding and unifying a people which fell to him demanded a singularity of purpose and a unique source of motivation, and it was in the spirit of Ruth, the soul of the desert's edge defied, that he found it. It was his inspiration as he led his people from Bethlehem to Jerusalem, theater ever after of history's greatest dramas.

# The Mountains Do Skip

*The mountains skip like rams, and the hills like young sheep...*

Psalm 114

Not a soul stirs in the mountainous wilderness of Judea during the sun-baked heat of the day. On the shimmering horizon, flocks of sheep graze languidly...or are they mere boulders? One cannot tell. In color and form, one is indistinguishable from the other.

Only when the sun dips low, and life resumes its pace, does the rhythm of the land reveal itself. The rocks and the sheep appeared before as one. Now one rises up from the stoney pillow of the other and the crests begin to heave and flow. The shepherd is leading home the flock, which just moments before was as still as the air.

Back to the corral come these lightly stepping, long-eyed creatures. They spill in careful streams along the well-worn paths which they have cut into the slope with geometric precision, which before had seemed like rings mysteriously etched around the slopes by some giant hand. They are a testimony: to the endless search of the flocks for food and water, and to the faithful shepherd leading them home at day's end.

You have never seen the mountains skip until you have seen the hills awaken at dusk, with the flocks' journey home.

*Sheep grazing in the Judean wilderness,
turned green by winter rain*

JNF Archives

*Cultivation at the Sataf
Spring in the Judean Hills*

JNF Archives

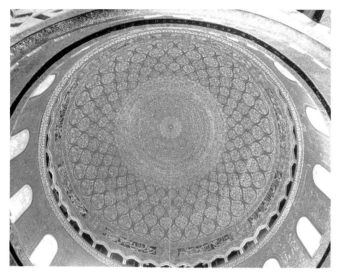

*Interior of the Dome of the Rock, built on Jerusalem's Temple Mount in 691 C.E., to commemorate the Prophet Mohammed's ascension to heaven. It is the third holiest place in the world for Muslims*
Palphot

*An aerial view of Jerusalem's Old City shows the Kidron and Hinnom Valleys protecting the city on the east and the southwest, while the northern approach has no natural defenses*
Government Press Office

*View of Mt. Zion from the east. On the summit is the Dormition Abbey, crowned by a black triangular roof, and flanked on the left by a small mineret, the site of King David's tomb. Midway down the mountain is the Church of Peter in Galicantu*
Aharon Vamosh

*Test of endurance: cultivation on the edge of the Judean wilderness*
JNF Archives

*Notre Dame de France, today a pilgrims' hostel, located outside the Old City's New Gate*

Miriam Feinberg Vamosh

*Russian Orthodox Church of Mary Magdelene on the Mount of Olives*

Ministry of Tourism Archives

# The Fruit of the Land

*I will sing for the one I love*
*A song about his vineyard.*
*My loved one had a vineyard*
*On a fertile hillside.*

Isaiah, Chapter 5

The curved crowns of the weathered hills flash by too swiftly. An image fixed on film can never touch the soul the way these hills do, in their stark reality. Choked with dust, they can only whisper hoarsely of another age, long since passed, when once they sweated under a mantle of soil and gave birth to burgeoning grapes and olives. From these the people of Judah pressed wine and oil, the mainstay of their lives. So many hillsides lie wasted now, emaciated; their skeletal frame protruding at every turn.

The fruit of the Land was crushed for a blessing; its people, in exile, crushed for a curse. The remnants flowed down from their homes on the crest, down into the valley where the soil rested, trapped and blooming. These still-fertile vines and groves stand greenly by the broken terraces of their barren sisters. They bring us homeward to the song of the vineyard, the love of the farmer for his Land, and the eternity of the Promise.

## Green Galilee

The palms are a waving friendly green. The breeze from the lake bids them welcome.

The terebinths are a pale and spikey green — in vain they attempt to ward off the climbing, hungry goats.

The stately green of the cypress is darkest of all, gravely reaching up to heaven.

The spritely green of the newly sprouted winter wheat is the lightest, not yet hiding the brownness of its bed beneath.

The slopes are a hesitant green. Soon they will become bold, for the first rain has burst the seeds laid in the parched and dry summer earth.

Shadowy green is the eternal olive, now gray in the morning glare, now blue with the kiss of the afternoon sun.

The new growth of the citrus groves is lemony green, brazenly imitating the ripening fruit below.

The redolent long green fingers are the eucalyptus, beckoning the traveller to their shade.

The Poinsianna trees are a proud green. They flaunt their flaming flowers, nodding and laughing at the wind as it passes.

Emerald-bright are the green lawns of the kibbutz, cultivated with care. Here children romp, or lie lazily, lost in daydreams.

In endless nuances, Galilee celebrates the hue of life.

## Olive Grove

All paths lead to the olive press, says the ancient adage. And though the paths have long since overgrown and the grove become silent, a touch of the great black basin, carved from the iron-hard volcanic rock, hot in the midday sun, can still conjure up a vibrant vision of those bygone days. The village women, undulating under carefully balanced baskets bearing the season's riches, approach the press. Each lays her burden in turn into the basin. The millstone revolves, driven endlessly by a tethered donkey, crushing the olives and releasing the virgin oil. From here the pulp is gathered to be placed between round flat baskets stacked in a column and pressed into oil by a tightly turned massive screw.

In Aramaic, a near-forgotten language, the word for olive press is "gat-shamna". Greek translations of the New Testament have rendered it "gethsemane". The centuries have divested this word of its original meaning; utter it now and images of betrayal, despair, appear. But not in this clearing near the grove. Here, the gathering is joyful. There is family talk, of romantic alliances and forthcoming births, and the last of the harvesting of summer fruits. Autumn has descended on the Land with a near imperceptible chill that moistens the afternoon breeze. The olives hang heavy and have begun to darken.

The harvesters reflect their joy at the fullness of the yield, for olive oil is a staple of their lives. Rich or poor, none could be without it. It was light, warmth, healing, and the ultimate symbol of royalty and consecration. They had one name for God's elect: "The anointed". The chosen one was anointed with olive oil, and they prayed that as the olive oil was absorbed into his skin, so divine attributes would be absorbed into his being.

The oil press tells a tale, thousands of years old, a tale of the heart-beat of the Land. The same trees which yielded their fruit to the press ten centuries ago will once again bear fruit, this year and next, and a thousand years hence with undiminished vigor. This most biblical of foliage has a special power. But the trees are of modest height and unremarkable color, and in the silence of the grove one must devote the quietest of moments to contemplation of the trees in order to divine the source of that power and their unique attraction.

Wait until a breeze stirs the leaves. Understand at that moment how the sages could have likened only the leaves of the olive to Sarah's joyous visage upon learning that she will bear Isaac: "her face shone like the olive tree". It is almost hidden, this arboreal luminescence. But when the wind stirs the leaves, it breaks forth in a shimmering sliver which wafts through the grove like the floating veil of a bride.

Contemplate its strength. Jeremiah taught the lesson of its noble contours: to him, Israel at its best was "an olive tree, leafy and fair". The sinews of its trunk are contorted as if struggling to lead to maturity one or the other of the offshoots appearing from its massive, cloven center. These youngsters are masters of survival. Though separated from the parent tree, with neither soil or water to sustain them, they will remain vital long after other species will have weakly surrendered their claim to life.

Psalm 128 imagines these saplings clustered around the tree as children faithfully surrounding their father: "Your sons will be like olive shoots around your table. Thus is the man blessed who fears the Lord". In all of the natural world, only the olive could so perfectly represent the greatest reward of the righteous — a close-knit family.

As much for the passionate poetry of its form as for its fruit, the olive tree won high regard in the eyes of the ancients. The old olive tree is an indomitable survivor, its oil the emblem of sovereignty and luxury, vehicle of security and good cheer. The olive tree is a true allegory of human aspirations.

## A Crusader's Prayer

My dear brothers,

I pray that this letter finds its way to you by the spring. The grip of winter is still upon us, here in the Holy Land, and at times like these, when I am nearly overcome with the crippling swelling of joints that have increasingly plagued me over the years, I fear that this will be the last of my letters to you, faithful correspondents across the sea.

All the brothers of our house are in good health, God be praised, and we are busily engaged in reestablishing ourselves. Do you know of the great changes that have taken place among us? The roads back to you are long and treacherous, so that I fear my previous letters may not have reached you. We have been living in the ruined buildings on the slope of Mount Tabor and we have undertaken to restore the large holdings here, abandoned after the latest incursion of the Saracens. Not all of the brothers were pleased when we received word to move from Acre to Mt. Tabor. I am afraid the attractions of the city were too much to their taste. Ships are constantly departing, bearing great riches, silks and spices, the sweet juice known here as "succar", and fine works of glass, so popular among the Venetians. The incoming ships are crowded with pilgrims, weary and often ill from the rigors of their journey. Much of our work was with these newcomers, doctoring, sheltering, and showing them the safest roads to the blessed shrines.

Indeed a wondrous city, dear brothers, but I was relieved to leave it, for plague is rampant, and death and disease were our constant companions. The streets are filthy, and it was all we could do to keep the stench from rising and penetrating our house through the latticed windows. Some of the brothers wished for window glass like that of noblemen, to keep the stench from our nostrils. Of course, our vows of poverty preclude such luxury, nor may we set ourselves apart from the miseries of those we are sworn to serve.

But now, safely ensconced within our new home, we have been working night and day to restore the site of our Lord's Transfiguration to its former glory. Our efforts have not been in vain, and it seems that each day our holdings grow greener, our stone fences more secure. I wish you could see the magnificent sights revealed from the summit of Tabor. I have spent many hours dwelling over the Song of Deborah, for wherever I cast my eye I come upon some mountain, river, or plain of which she sang. Beneath me, I see the battlefield of her victory over the Canaanites. I look east to the mountains of Gilead, birthplace of our beloved St. Elijah, through whom God has revealed His ideal of a monk. To the south is green Ein Harod, where Gideon chose his soldiers to fight against the Midianites. Naturally, I follow the dictates of our bishops, as do you, that our flock must learn of the glory of Christ only as it is revealed in the New Testament. But I cannot help wondering if we do them a disservice by keeping these marvelous Old Testament tales to ourselves.

By now most of you know me only through letters — I wonder if anyone amongst you remembers when I took up the cross, so many years ago. Those days are still vivid in my memory: the tumultuous days of the siege upon Jerusalem, the sight of our brave knights marching around the ramparts as Joshua did at Jericho. I still shiver at the memory of the apparition that led us to victory, of St. George, to whose everlasting glory the walls of Jerusalem finally crumbled.

But to this day I have carried within my heart the shame I witnessed the day our forces entered the Holy City: the killing, the pillaging, the murder of Jews, Saracens, and of our fellow-Christians, whom we did not recognize as such because they wore beards. I have never shared this indelible sense of our disgrace with anyone, and it is only because I know in my heart that by the time this letter reaches you I will be with the Lord that I am able to reveal it now.

Since that massacre, and most certainly from the moment Baldwin was crowned king in the city where our True King was born in the most humble of circumstances, I have been assailed with misgivings. I fear that our efforts have been futile, for when our enemy succeeds in uniting its warring factions, not even the strongest of fortresses will save us. In all of my days in the Holy Land, I have never been more certain than now that our mission will ultimately come to a dismal end.

And I know why it is so. Though many among us love the Savior passionately, we have not loved the Land which nurtured Him, but have used it to enrich ourselves. We have not loved the People from whom our Savior sprang, but have plundered and murdered them. And we have shown no compassion for Christians born of the Land, who alone carried the torch for generations among the infidels; we have enslaved them.

My soul and my doubts will soon be laid to rest. I hope that from Heaven I will someday watch Christians come to this Land with a pure heart and a renewal of the spirit, which we have so tragically lost. Work towards that day, my brothers, and pray for me as I pray for you.

Your brother in Christ

## The Valley of Ayalon

During every age, no matter who the conquerer, the Land was his only if he mastered the mountains running like a spine down its back. At the Valley of Ayalon, western gateway to the Judean Hills, he would meet the crucial test of his martial skills. Many an army thundered across the seacoast and entered the Valley of Ayalon as though it were an open door. But the hills on the eastern edge of the valley, which had so generously given of their soil to make it fertile, became stern and unyielding in their protection of the highlands beyond, and resolutely closed ranks against the invader. No matter how unencumbered its coastal passage had been, no force could breach these mountains without heavy losses. No force was prepared for the conspiracy between these mountains and their defenders secreted in the tortuous passes.

In a long-ago pre-dawn chill, the armies of the Amorites amassed in the valley to do battle against the Gibeonites and their new champion, Joshua. The column of enemy soldiers snaked its way painfully up the twisting defiles. They were trapped: as Joshua stood high above them, the sun rose behind him, at his command becoming a lethal weapon. Arrested in its heavenly course, it burned relentlessly in the eyes of Joshua's predators, until they were forced to turn and flee down the narrow defile of Beth Horon leading back to Ayalon. The moon did not set that day at its appointed hour, but rather tarried to watch Joshua manipulate heaven and earth to scatter his foes.

The tale of Joshua's victory here resounded through the ages, to nourish and strengthen a people on the threshold of its history. Perhaps this story inspired a later leader, of humble origins, turned soldier in the service of his people. For Judah Maccabee was also to make use of the valley's treacherous passageways to strike a fatal blow at the mightiest military machine of his day. Judah's triumph over the Seleucid Greeks, in the very same place where Joshua had fought eleven centuries before, opened the way for the glorious rededication of the Temple in Jerusalem.

From the days of the Bible to the days of the British, army after army crossed the Ayalon. The valley watched them bleed and die here, in sharp contrast to the verdant tranquility of the surrounding fields. And nowhere were the birthpangs of the State of Israel more agonizing than in this place.

A great fortress watches over the valley — a fitting reminder of its turbulent history. It stands in isolation on a barren hillock, its sulking, angular form providing no relief or distraction from its gray facade.

The fortress stares out stonily across a small divide at its nearest neighbor, the Latrun Monastery. In the face of such beauty, warfare is almost forgotten. It is the antithesis of the fiery stronghold across the landscape. Russet roof tiles brought from over the sea are lovingly placed over porticos of elegantly carved Judean stone, while delicate arabesques arch gracefully over the windows.

When the gentle Trappist brothers who built the Monastery pledged their future to this Land, did they know that they would bring their arbors to fruition in fields so drenched in blood? In their prayers, do they beg release from the din and clash of ghostly armies they cannot help but hear at every turn? How did they fare when this latest generation's challenge for the valley locked the adversaries in deadly struggle outside their tranquil door?

Fortress of armor, fortress of faith. So subtle the distance between them. Bastion of belief, and of belligerence. Who will tell the final tale of Ayalon?

# Mount Carmel

*...Now summon the people from all over Israel to meet me on Mount Carmel. And bring the four hundred and fifty prophets of Baal and the four hundred prophets of Asherah that eat at Jezebel's table.*

*So Ahab sent word throughout all Israel and assembled the prophets on Mount Carmel. Elijah went before the people and said,*

*How long will you waver between two opinions? If the Lord is God, follow him; but if Baal is God, follow him.*

I Kings 18:19-21

Legend teaches us that when the time came for God to choose a mountain from which to present the Ten Commandments, the mountains of the Holy Land appeared in turn before Him, vying for the honor. God refused Carmel, so goes the tale, for idol worship had defiled its heights.

Carmel rises up gently along the coast, riding the swells of the plain of Sharon. Then, like the prow of some great ship, she heads out to sea. Figurehead of the Land, she forever turns her rocky cheeks to the salty breeze, for from her perch above the water she will be the first to spy the rainclouds after each long and thirsty summer.

Blessed with plentiful rainfall in its season, Carmel is true to its name, "Garden of God". Carmel is forever green, home to a species of oak whose leaves scarcely wither before they fall and whose branches are never truly bare. Before the last leaf of autumn has drifted to the ground, the buds of new growth are there to take their place. Acorns take root in the still verdant carpet at the base of each sturdy tree. Many kinds of animals seek out the protection of the thickets: wild boar, deer, a dozen species of

To the ancients, Carmel symbolized nature's abundance. The prophet Isaiah called Carmel "excellent", and the Song of Songs created an ideal of beauty incomparable to earthly woman, likening the head crowning this vision to the perfection of Mt. Carmel.

God had revealed himself to the Israelites in an environment far different from this. The stark Sinai desert with its monochrome peaks and the unbroken tension of its horizons, its freezing nights and burning days, epitomized the uncompromising oneness of God. But in Canaan, in places such as Carmel, the people discovered a Land where nature rejoiced in endless variety. They could not accept that one single force had created such bounty. Their heads were turned by the religion of the Canaanites: with one god for the oak trees, another to give life to the animals, and still another to send the rain in its season. And so at Carmel they called the oak trees "sacred", and from beneath their boughs they made sacrifices to Baal and Asherah. At Carmel, land of plenty, the people forgot the God of Sinai.

But the God of Sinai is Lord of the Universe, and He did not forget His people. A never-ending dry season cursed the Land. Carmel, ever green, would wither and bear most unmistakably the mark of Divine displeasure. The people had allowed the excellence of Carmel to lead them astray; therefore that excellence would be denied them.

When Elijah set up the altar of the Lord on the mountain where his people had turned away from God, he knew that none other than this same mountain would do as the site of their return. And nothing but fire could be the instrument of that return. Through fire, the people at Carmel, like Moses at Horeb before the burning bush, would acknowledge the undeniable power of God.

In the very place where the actions of this people had provoked a disturbance in the

cycle of nature, balance had now been restored. Purified by fire, the valleys of Carmel rang with the cry,
*The Lord He is God, The Lord He is God!*
*...The sky grew black with clouds, and the wind rose.*

The covenant had been renewed, and the rains of blessing fell.

*The southern shore of the Sea of Galilee, near Kibbutz Degania*
JNF Archives

*An ancient olive oil press with olive trees in the foreground, at Katzrin in the Golan*
Miriam Feinberg Vamosh

*View of Mount Tabor in the Jezreel Valley*

JNF Archives

*The Valley of Ayalon from the southwest. At left, the Latrun Fortress built by the British. At right, the Trappist Monastery of Latrun*

Roy Brody

*View of Mount Carmel*

JNF Archives

*Blossoming almond trees near St. John in the Wilderness Monastery in the Judean Hills*

# Trees of Hope

*When you lay siege to a city...do not destroy its trees...because you can eat of their fruit. Do not cut them down. Are the trees of the field people, that you should besiege them?*

Deuteronomy 20:19

Among the Biblical ordinances governing the conquest of cities and the uprooting of peoples, a line of poetry lies hidden, as delicate as the winter branches etched against the white Judean sky. We are startled by the simplicity of the question, confounded at the comparison between our restless acquisitive selves and the tranquil trees of the field.

Legend relates that the farmers in the Valley of Kidron vied with each other over the rivulets that provided water for their trees, water flowing down from the Temple Mount, tinged with the blood of the sacrifices. God blessed the fruit nurtured from the worship of His Holy Name. Perhaps. But the generations have wrought destruction here, and the Land has roiled with their ancient anger. From the blood of human folly, soaking the very soil to their roots, the trees cannot benefit.

Spare the fruit trees, spare them! They must blossom and bear fruit in their season. They are the hope for the future of a wounded Land. Gray stones, culled from ancient disarray, climb the hills in terraced walls, embracing the high fields row upon row. Plum, pomegranate, apples and almonds: sustenance of our ancestors next to brash newcomers from distant lands. They splash the hillsides with joyous pastels in the spring. They never know mourning. In summer their boughs hang heavy, even when there is none to gather their harvest. In winter they gladly relinquish their branches to the pruning, to warm a thousand hearths.

A great love was to be cherished between this land and its inhabitants. We were to love its bounty more than we hated our enemy. We were to tend the trees with a reverence and gentleness we could not feel towards humanity. We were not to abuse the trees, even as our wars raged around us.

The trees are a sign. In time, perhaps they will teach the battle-weary of this Land to emulate their nobility. When we desist from destruction, the trees will remain, and the time will have arrived to eat of their fruit.